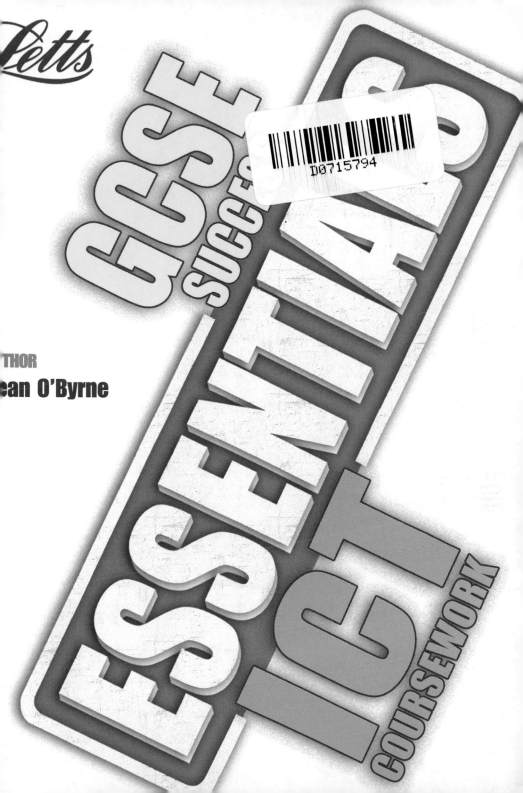

Letts

GCSE SUCCESS ESSENTIALS

ICT COURSEWORK

AUTHOR

Sean O'Byrne

D0715794

Every effort has been made to contact the holders of copyright material, but if any have been inadvertently overlooked the publishers will be pleased to make the necessary arrangements at the first opportunity.

Published by Letts Educational
The Chiswick Centre
414 Chiswick High Road
London W4 5TF
tel: 020 89963333
fax: 020 87428390
e-mail: mail@lettsed.co.uk
website: www.letts-education.com

Letts Educational Limited is a division of Granada Learning Limited, part of Granada Plc.

Text © Sean O'Byrne 2005.
Design and illustration © Letts Educational Ltd 2005.

First published 2005

ISBN 1844190455

The author asserts his moral right to be identified as the author of this work.

British Library Cataloguing in Publication Data

A catalogue record for this book is available from the British Library.

Microsoft Access®, Microsoft Excel®, Microsoft FrontPage®, Microsoft Internet Explorer®, Microsoft Office®, Microsoft Outlook Express®, Microsoft PowerPoint®, Microsoft Publisher®, Microsoft Word®, Microsoft Visual Basic®, MS-DOS Debug®, are registered trademarks of Microsoft Corporation. Screen shots reprinted by permission from Microsoft Corporation.

Diagrams on page 24 supplied by kind permission of NCC Education, Manchester.

Cover design by Big Top.

Commissioned by Cassandra Birmingham

Project management for Letts by Julia Swales

Edited by The Cambridge Editorial Partnership

Design and project management by Ken Vail Graphic Design, Cambridge

Printed and bound in Italy.

Introduction

Getting started

Topic areas

Projects

Example database project

Contents

Introduction

This book is a guide showing you how to use software skills in order to organise good projects and get the highest marks possible.

For more guidance on how to develop these software skills, see *Letts Success for Schools KS3 Framework Course,* books 1–4.

GCSE coursework

When you decide to do a GCSE ICT course, you need to realise the importance of coursework right from the start. Whichever specification you are doing and whether you are doing the full or the short course, it is worth 60% of your assessment.

Clearly, 60% is a lot! Very few other subjects place so much importance on coursework. There are advantages and disadvantages to this.

ADVANTAGES

- If you take care over your coursework, you will have less to get stressed about when the exam comes – you will already have done most of the work.
- You can produce your coursework over quite a long period.
- You can keep refining your work until you are happy with it.
- If your teacher assesses your work accurately you can get a pretty good idea about what grade you will get, so there should be no nasty surprises. You could have a grade 'C' or maybe even a 'B' before you pick up your pen in the written exam.

DISADVANTAGES

- Some students find it very hard to keep going with coursework.
- It is sometimes difficult to choose a good topic.
- You have to be able to work on your own. If you need constant nagging to get the coursework done, you will probably not do very well.
- Some students react better to learning the work and taking exams.

This book is intended to help you make good choices and put all the right things into your coursework so that you get the best marks possible.

What is GCSE coursework for?

ICT is very much a practical subject. It is intended to give you knowledge and experience of a range of tools and techniques. Of course, you have to know a lot of theory for the exam, but you also have to demonstrate that you can actually make use of ICT resources in order to **produce something**. What you produce and how well you present this helps the examiners to decide what grade to give you.

It is important to understand what we mean by **producing something**. You can:

- use a computer to make something such as a document or a spreadsheet, or

- use a computer to produce a **system** – probably for someone else to use.

You need to be clear which of these approaches you are using at any particular time. The requirements depend upon the different awarding bodies, but a system for others to use is generally considered to be higher level work.

Know your specification

This varies quite a lot between the awarding bodies. The differences are mostly to do with exactly how you produce your work and present it. There are many guiding principles that apply, no matter what specification you are doing.

You will certainly get a better mark if you present your coursework **exactly** as it is laid down in **your** specification.

Types of coursework

There are three basic types of coursework and they are mixed and matched in different ways by the awarding bodies.

They all require you to:

- demonstrate that you can use a variety of software
- write documentation to show that you understand what you are doing and can communicate your work to others.

Most GCSE projects centre on one or just a limited range of software applications. One awarding body specifies that you have to do a spreadsheet project and a database project. Others give you a free choice.

1 Set tasks

These are laid down by the awarding body. They set out specific tasks to carry out, based on a scenario that is different each year. As with all coursework, it has to be fully documented.

2 Short tasks chosen by the student

These are also intended to demonstrate that you can solve a problem by using software. You choose a scenario that interests you and you produce a solution then write suitable documentation for it. Sometimes these are called a **portfolio**.

3 Projects

These are where, ideally, you solve a substantial problem from start to finish, **for someone else**. You identify a situation that can be handled by a computer solution and progress through well-defined stages to produce a system to solve the problem.

Nearly all the full course specifications require projects although they vary slightly in the exact content required and the amount of work expected. For example, the Edexcel coursework consists of four quite short items of this type, with no other coursework. AQA Specification A, OCR Specification A and WJEC require one larger project together with other types of coursework.

Choosing topics for coursework

Most project work is based on:

- choosing a problem that can be solved by using a computer
- investigating and analysing the problem
- designing a solution
- producing the solution
- evaluating how successful it has been.

Often, the hardest part is deciding what topic to choose. Getting this right is vital. If you choose well, the rest of the project can almost 'do itself', because the steps to be taken are fairly clear. Get this wrong and you may find that you are struggling for ages without really being sure what you need to do. So, make sure you do some clear thinking from the start.

Getting the level right

NOT TOO SIMPLE

GCSE allows students to achieve a wide range of grades.

1 You can produce the clearest, most beautifully laid out project imaginable, but if the underlying ICT work is trivial, you cannot get the highest marks.

2 In the same way, if you do all sorts of clever things but leave out lots of the documentation, then, again, you will not do as well as you could.

3 Some students don't like the subject very much or maybe they just don't want to find the time to do all sorts of complex work. That's a decision that you might make. If so, you have to be clear about it and realise that you are probably only going for a maximum of grade C.

4 If you are going for the top grades, you must make sure that your project includes some reasonably clever work. Later, we shall look at what that means for different types of project. For the moment, bear in mind that a

Tip

To get the highest marks on an ICT project:

- all the sections must be written up properly, clearly and thoroughly
- the project must be quite ambitious.

top grade project will probably contain a **range** of techniques rather than just one. This can mean that you use more than one type of software in order to produce a complete solution to a problem.

5 Some examining bodies award different bands of marks according to the level of difficulty of the project. Also, a simple project will automatically get lower marks because it has less scope for a thorough analysis and design than a more ambitious one.

6 You **can** make a project by producing a single, one-off solution such as making a spreadsheet to work out the costs of **your** holiday or producing one week's edition of a newsletter. It is much better, however, to make something that is reusable for someone else so that the product you make can be applied again and again in different circumstances.

NOT TOO COMPLEX

Moderators always see some projects that they describe as 'OTT' – over the top! These are the projects which are 5 cm thick, beautifully bound and weigh a tonne! They often wonder 'how can this student have time to do all the other subjects as well.' If you want to produce a spectacular blockbuster, containing all manner of fantastic and clever techniques then fine. You might have a lot of fun doing it and you will quite possibly also get an A*, but don't neglect your other subjects and make sure you leave some time in your life for having fun. You can get an A* with much less work.

So, you have to get the balance right when planning your project: a system to work out the cost of buying ten items is not likely to be worth much; a new operating system to rival Windows will probably not get done by the deadline!

Tip You will be spending quite a lot of time on your coursework so it will help if you choose a topic that can keep you interested.

The user

When choosing a topic if helps if you have someone else's interests in mind. The user can normally be anyone, such as:

- a friend who may want an easy way to keep details of a CD collection
- a family member who wants some help in working out the cost of a wedding
- a small business that wants a financial record-keeping solution to help with tax returns
- a teacher who may be in need of an electronic mark book
- as a last resort – you yourself may want to produce a revision timetable for a year's work.

It is **much** easier to follow a project through if you have (at least in your imagination) someone else's point of view. In fact, in many cases, you cannot get maximum credit unless you show interaction with your user or 'client'.

ADVANTAGES AND DISADVANTAGES OF DIFFERENT USERS

1 Solutions aimed at small businesses or other organisations tend to be the most successful in terms of completing all the sections required. This is because there is likely to be plenty going on that can be made more accurate or labour saving.

2 Solutions for individuals can sometimes be trivial. This is because their requirements may be limited to just a few calculations or documents, or maybe just storing a small number of names and addresses.

Tip Remember that some specifications require your project to include a user guide. You can't do this if you don't have a user!

3 Major solutions for big businesses are going to be unrealistic at GCSE level because there is just so much to consider to make sure that a solution fits in with all their many activities.

Getting the quality right

It can be difficult to know just how much to do and how much depth is needed. Don't forget, you want to get the best possible grade without crowding out the rest of your life. There are some tricks to help you with this.

LOOK AT OTHER PROJECTS BEFORE YOU START

This is one of the most important things to do. Your school probably has a collection of old projects done by previous students. You should look at some of these to:

- get ideas for topics
- see the sort of depth required
- get some idea of how they are marked.

There is no limit to the number of topics suitable for project work. Some ideas that have been used are:

- a stock-control system for a shop, restaurant, veterinary or doctor's surgery, warehouse or factory
- a membership system for any club, leisure centre, library or amateur dramatic society
- a costing system to find out the viability of a proposed holiday, social event or dance
- a set of related documents for an organisation, such as headed notepaper, invoices, till receipts, web pages, business cards – preferably produced automatically
- an ordering system to ensure that an organisation has all the stock it needs without tying up too much cash in unnecessary items. This could be for a shop, a farm, a decorator, a plumber or any other business
- matching customers to their wants such as in a dating agency, an estate agency or a travel agent
- tracking systems for sales, stock market performance or weather.

Some will be good examples of what **not** to do! You can learn a lot from bad projects. Some common mistakes are:

- leaving out whole sections
- not producing diagrams and flow charts
- not relating enough to the user's needs
- poor presentation
- bad English
- not dividing the work into sections.

The awarding bodies also produce specimen projects. These are usually real ones that may have been 'doctored' in some way to make a point. There are various ways of getting hold of these.

- As booklets. Your teacher can get these from the awarding body.
- Some are available on the awarding bodies' websites.
- Teachers normally go to training meetings in order to learn how to guide students and mark the work properly. These meetings provide specimen work at different levels. Ask your teacher if you can see some.

DON'T WORRY ABOUT BEING ORIGINAL

Students often want to do something challenging that is not as boring as some of the projects that they have seen. This is all well and good if it helps you to keep interested. However, the main thing you want is to get a good grade and there are plenty of 'tried and tested' topics that make a reliable framework for showing off what you can do.

> Remember – you get most of your credit for your documentation. If your project is so unusual that the documentation is difficult, you may lose out. Grinding out yet another system for a video rental shop may be unoriginal, but at least you will know what to put in it.

BUT DON'T DO EXACTLY THE SAME AS EVERYONE ELSE!

Your project is supposed to be **your** choice. Some schools and colleges give the students a scenario and ask them all to do a project on that theme. **This is bad advice!** There is a danger that the moderator will downgrade work that is common to a number of projects.

Worse still, some teachers actually provide a template and ask the students to adjust it slightly to make it a bit individual. **This is terrible advice!**

If you can – avoid being misled like this! If your work has a lot in common with everyone else in your centre, you run the risk of only being credited for the bits that are different. Worse still, if there are large chunks of identical material, you may be heading for disqualification from the exam and possibly other exams as well.

INVOLVE THE USER

See **The user** on page 9.

In real life, a software developer works with the client to produce a solution that is really helpful. Remember – if the client doesn't like the result, the developer might not get paid! Therefore, the user should be involved every step of the way.

Tip The best projects copy real life.

USE A VARIETY OF TECHNIQUES

Some projects fall down because they are too simple. Avoid this by making sure that whatever software you use, you make the most of its capabilities. By the time you do GCSE coursework, you will have lots of experience of lots of types of software. Think of some of the less obvious things you did. See if you can incorporate some of them into the project.

Tip

Good projects include lots of feedback and suggestions from the client. Put them in wherever you can.

GET TO KNOW THE MARK SCHEME

Your project is marked according to a mark scheme. Your teacher should mark your work according to the mark scheme.

Just in case your teacher has a different view from others, some work is sampled by people called 'moderators'. They are employed by the awarding bodies to make sure that everybody gets marked in the same way. If the marks from a school or college are generally too high or too low, the moderator will make adjustments.

Presentation

There are no marks in the mark schemes for presentation as such. But presentation is **very important**. A well-presented project is logical and all the necessary parts are there.

You have to impress the reader with your:
- clarity
- completeness
- cleverness.

Your audience

You must know your reader and write the report accordingly. You have two readers to impress. It helps if you understand who these people are and what motivates them.

YOUR TEACHER

In the first instance, your project will be read and marked by your teacher. Your teacher will have (or should have) watched your project develop. Be ready for the possibility that the moderator may not agree with the teacher's mark. Don't relax and take any less effort with your theory revision just because you get a good project mark. You may be moderated down.

THE MODERATOR

The moderator will read a sample of the projects from a centre. It may include yours. It helps to know a thing or two about moderators.

- They have no particular interest in whether a candidate does well or badly.
- They have hundreds of projects to read in a very short time.
- They don't get paid much so they want to work fast!
- What they want most is not to have to adjust the marks of a centre – this just means more paperwork.
- But – if they see bad work that has been marked high, they get upset. (They rarely see good work that has been marked low!)

You should think about the moderator right through your project. What he or she wants most of all is to understand what you are doing **as fast as possible** and check that you have covered everything you should in a thorough and efficient way.

Tip

Remember – you want to communicate **fast** and **clearly**.

Break it up

The most effective way to get your point across in a written report is to present things in small, easy to notice sections. It is best if these follow a logical order. There are some standard ways of doing this.

HEADINGS

Be generous with headings and sub-headings. We have already noted that the awarding body provides five or six headings that you really must use. Within these, feel free to make more sub-headings of your own.

USE BULLET POINTS

Nobody wants a project to be a great work of literature, or worse a very boring piece of writing. There is a job to be done and reported on. The reader of your project wants to know:

- what you are doing
- how you intend to do it
- whether you did do it
- how it turned out.

Remember, an ICT project is usually about producing a product **for a client**. Right from the outset, it is necessary to establish what the client wants. These wants can be expressed as a rough list. Throughout the project, you will need to refer to this list again and again so that you can be sure that what you are doing is what the client wants.

WHITE SPACE

If you want to communicate quickly – and you do – you need plenty of white space. This is the space that separates paragraphs, sections and diagrams so that each stage in your report is absolutely clear. Don't write long chunks of text. This makes it very difficult to get the point quickly.

Other presentation points

SENTENCE STRUCTURE

Your sentences should be short and punchy. Don't ramble on. Re-read what you have said after you have written it. Can it be shortened and still say the same thing?

DIAGRAMS

Use lots of them. They can often communicate what you want to say more

quickly than words. They also add variety to what
the reader sees. Some diagrams are best done
by hand. It is often easier to make designs
on the computer but some moderators don't
like that.

Tip

Some of the
awarding bodies
specifically look
for hand-drawn
diagrams in the
design stage.

FLOW CHARTS

In ICT projects, flow charts have a special place.

You can do these easily with your word
processor or maybe you have special software to do
them. Do use them when you can but only when appropriate. They should be
proper flow charts such as:

■ data flow diagrams

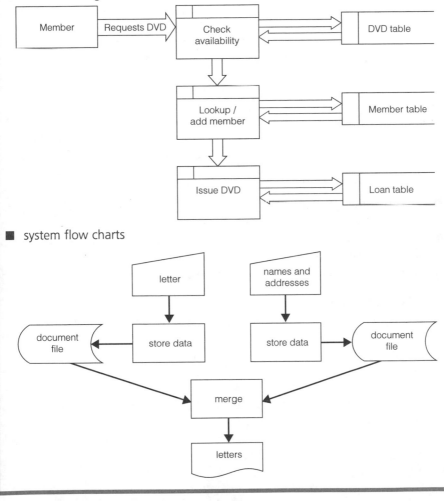

■ system flow charts

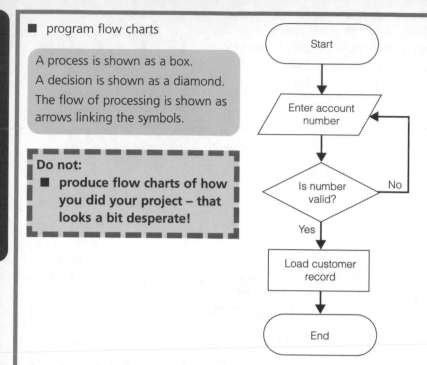

- program flow charts

A process is shown as a box.
A decision is shown as a diamond.
The flow of processing is shown as arrows linking the symbols.

Do not:
- **produce flow charts of how you did your project – that looks a bit desperate!**

Flow charts should use the correct shapes and the text in them should be correct and **brief**. Put one or two words in each box such as 'customer file' or 'find overdue videos' but certainly **not** long sentences.

FONTS AND FONT SIZES
- Projects written in big fonts look as if the student is desperately trying to fill as much space as possible with a bad project.
- Fancy fonts should also be avoided. They look childish and always seem to be used by candidates who produce very trivial projects.
- Stick to a plain font such as Times Roman or Arial.

JUSTIFICATION
- It is your choice whether to fully justify your text, but it is probably better not to.
- Left-aligned text tends to be easier to read.

SPELLING AND GRAMMAR
- This is very important. Some coursework credits 5% of the marks for 'spelling, punctuation and grammar'.
- Bad spelling and grammar give a generally 'amateurish' feel to a project that is usually reflected in other aspects of it.
- Do a spell check.

TECHNICAL TERMS

Good projects use technical terms correctly where needed. Your work does not have to be so full of jargon that it is unreadable, but you are expected to 'know your stuff'.

ANNOTATION

- **Everything** should be clear.
- Diagrams and printouts should never leave the reader wondering 'what is this?'
- Add notes to explain **everything**.

PAGE NUMBERS

- These really help to find your way around.
- They are more or less vital when referring to the results of any tests that you carry out.
- They give a good 'finished' feel to the work.

TABLE OF CONTENTS

- Most students don't do one of these, but it can help a lot in organising what you do.
- If your work is organised, it will be easy to read and more likely to gain you higher marks.

TO BIND OR NOT TO BIND?

- Comb binding certainly helps to improve the appearance of a project.
- You can present your work in a document wallet if you like, but it is better if it is a new one.

Comb binding is a way of securing loose pages using a piece of plastic with 'teeth' that fits into rectangular holes in the paper.

Do not:
- present your work in a ring binder – they get broken in the post to the moderator and the work goes everywhere. You can, however, use treasury tags to hold together hole-punched sheets.
- put your pages in plastic wallets – if there is one sheet per wallet, it makes the work heavy. If there are lots of sheets per wallet, it takes ages for the moderator to get them out and put them back and that makes him mad!

NAMES AND NUMBERS

Make sure that your work is clearly identified with:
- the title of the project
- your name
- your centre number
- your candidate number.

Some students put all this in a footer and that works well.

Identification

Some exam boards require you to have an 'identification section' in your project.

Any real-life project starts out with the need to identify the problem. This is where the analyst finds out:

- the background to the company or some other client
- what the problems are.

As far as GCSE coursework is concerned, the **identification section** is absolutely crucial to the success of the rest of the project. It fulfils two important purposes:

1 It helps you to focus exactly on what you will be doing later.

2 It communicates important first impressions to whoever marks and moderates your project. It must get across very quickly and clearly what is going to happen. A moderator looks at this section to make a few quick judgements about whether the project is likely to be clear and whether it is likely to be in enough depth.

GENERAL TIPS

- If your specification actually has the heading 'Identify' as one of the sections to be covered, make absolutely sure that you use the word as a main heading. This ensures that you cover everything and also helps the person who is marking your work.
- It is helpful if you also include some sub-headings. In the identify section, you are trying to nail down exactly what your work will include and also what it will not include. This is far better tackled in small bite-sized chunks.
- Long sections of text are to be avoided because they don't focus your mind on the things that need doing.

What goes into the Identify section?

TITLE

Give your work a title. This helps keep you focused on what it is about. It also helps your teacher to help you. When looking after lots of students, it is easy to forget who is doing what! A meaningful title helps everybody.

BACKGROUND

Tell the story of the business, organisation or individual who needs the solution. Again, this is to help you and others be clear about what is going on. What you say here depends on circumstances but you might include:

- the name of the business
- where it is located
- what it does (in brief)
- how big it is in terms of number of branches, number of employees, number of transactions per day or other things you can count or measure
- who are its customers or clients
- roughly – what aspect of the business needs a computer solution
- the position or the name of the person who wants the computer system.

THE CURRENT SYSTEM

If your project is about providing a new system to improve an old one, you should explain clearly, but briefly, how they do things at the moment. Make sure that you focus on a particular area.

Tip It is usually a mistake to try to take on too much. If you are producing a system for keeping track of renting out DVDs, you wouldn't include staff wages as well. Be clear about what you are leaving out.

THE PROBLEM

Someone needs a computer system. Why? Is there one already but it doesn't perform well enough? Is it a manual or a paper system?

The problem might be that the current system is inefficient. Typical reasons for needing a new computer system are:

- it takes too long to look up what is in stock (or some other job)
- records aren't up to date
- invoices aren't getting paid
- customers are kept waiting on the phone for too long
- the quality of advertising is poor
- files keep getting lost
- the overall image of the company is old fashioned.

It might be that the problem is not something that is being done badly at the moment. It may be that some entirely new job needs to be done, e.g.

- sales might be improved by selling on the Internet
- a new product has been launched and advertising is needed
- a school has introduced a new course and needs to timetable it
- a business is expanding and wants to work out the costs of new premises.

OBJECTIVES

Be clear about what the new system will achieve. It will help you a lot if you produce objectives as a bullet point list. Some specifications tell you how many objectives you need.

Good objectives are:

'The system will
- print a list of overdue invoices
- only accept valid product names
- match client with three potential 'dates' in the dating agency and send a suitable letter.'

All of these objectives can be checked for success.

Tip

Later, you will have to evaluate your success in meeting these objectives. Make sure that these are easy to check later on. It is not much help if an objective is vague such as 'the flyer will be attractive and colourful'. This is difficult to measure and will be a matter of opinion.

ALTERNATIVE SOLUTIONS

You need to look at more than one possible way of solving the problem. You should argue the case for using **reasonable** alternative examples of software. (Don't put in unrealistic choices here such as using a spreadsheet to produce a newsletter.) You may want to at least consider the case for sticking to a paper solution. You could set out the pros and cons for doing this, but don't follow that solution up or you will not have a project!

A good strategy is often to compare the merits of using a spreadsheet or database software to store and process a set of data.

We shall look at this in more detail later as this is very often a good way to decide how best to tackle a problem.

Check to see which section should include alternative solutions – this varies in different specifications.

You should give the pros and cons for a variety of approaches and you should argue the case for the method that you finally choose. The case must be based on matching the facilities of the software to the task in hand. It is not much help to say that you are using, say, Excel because it is the only spreadsheet software that you have available. You must also say something about its advantages for the task you want it to perform.

Analysis

This section is often done badly. Many students just don't know what to put in here. A poor analysis will affect the rest of the project.

It might help if you try to imagine each stage of the project being done by different people, as it probably would be in real life. The analysis is done by the systems analyst. This person does not need to bother with the details of things like program code and customising packages – he or she only needs to decide upon the main steps along the way.

What analysis is

- The breaking down of a problem into its component parts.
- A picture of what needs to be done.
- A schedule of when things need to be done.
- An overall plan and a statement of intent.

REQUIREMENTS SPECIFICATION

At the end of the analysis, you should come up with a bullet point list of the things that the client requires the system to do. This list must be consulted throughout the rest of the project so that you can check that everything is proceeding according to the client's requirements.

What analysis is not

Analysis is not the full details of what to do – that comes in the design.

What goes into the analysis

It helps if you think of sub-headings for the analysis section first. It gives you a structure to work to, and makes sure you cover all the necessary areas.

SOFTWARE

You may have already decided what software to use. In the analysis, give full details. The name and version number of the software and what aspects of it are important to the project. If you are using Excel, you might want to specify that you are going to use some of its built-in functions, its graph-plotting capabilities and some macros. You might also mention software other than the main choice, for example, you may want to mention the platform that the software requires.

The platform is the combination of hardware and operating system that is needed to run a particular application. For example, most projects will be on an Intel and Windows platform. The version of Windows can be mentioned – it is sometimes important in determining whether or not an application can run.

HARDWARE

Very many students neglect to put in any comments about the hardware. You can put yourself at an advantage by including this. Make sure that you say something better than just 'a computer and a printer'. Give the specifications of the system.

Activity

Visit a PC manufacturer's website such as www.dell.co.uk and look at the specifications of several suitable computer systems. Include things like the amount of RAM, clock speed and disk size. You may need more than one of some items. Find out the cost as well. Think of a reason why you need each of their specifications.

ANALYSIS SECTIONS

You will find it easier to do a good analysis if you break it up into sections. Here are some ideas for these sections. Feel free to add extra headings if they suit your particular project.

OUTPUT

Computer systems are developed to produce output that can be printed invoices, animated film on screen, or even a signal to a motor. This section needs to be quite extensive and carefully thought out.

First, decide what types of output will be needed.

1 Paper output
   This will often be lists, but it might be a publication, a report or graphs. Sketch out a rough plan of **each** document required.

2 Screen output
   This will normally be important if you are:

   a) doing an enquiry system where things are being looked up – such as a customer's bank account details where details will be shown on a screen

   b) making an on-screen display of some kind such as a website or multimedia show. (A school might need a PowerPoint display to show the activities of the ICT department on a screen on an open day.)

At the very least, list the screens that you will need. Ideally, add some rough sketches of their layouts.

3 Other output

Some projects will have motors or other actuators as output. Others might use sound output.

> An actuator is any hardware device that makes something happen in response to a signal. It may be a motor that opens a window or maybe an electromagnet that operates a switch, as in a relay.

You should feed back some of your ideas about output to the client and add some reactions and possibly some amendments in the light of the responses.

DATA REQUIRED

Make a list of all the data that you will need in order to get the outputs that you want. It might be a set of **names and addresses**, **prices**, **items in stock** or **the events that you want to put in a newsletter**. At this stage, it need not be perfectly organised, but you should try to think of everything.

DATA COLLECTION

Make some decisions about where the data will come from and make sure you outline these in your analysis.

- Will it be on forms that people fill in? If so, sketch one.
- Does the firm already have data-collection forms? If so, include one.
- Will the data be collected verbally from customers, maybe on the phone?
- Will it be gathered from websites or will it be collected automatically as in a data-logging experiment?

DATA FLOW

You will probably be producing a **system**. This is a set of interconnected resources and processes. You should draw diagrams to show how the data enters the system, flows through it and eventually leaves it. This is best done by drawing a proper **data flow diagram** and also **context diagrams**. Your data flow diagram will include such things as:

- people
- departments
- processes
- data stores (files/tables).

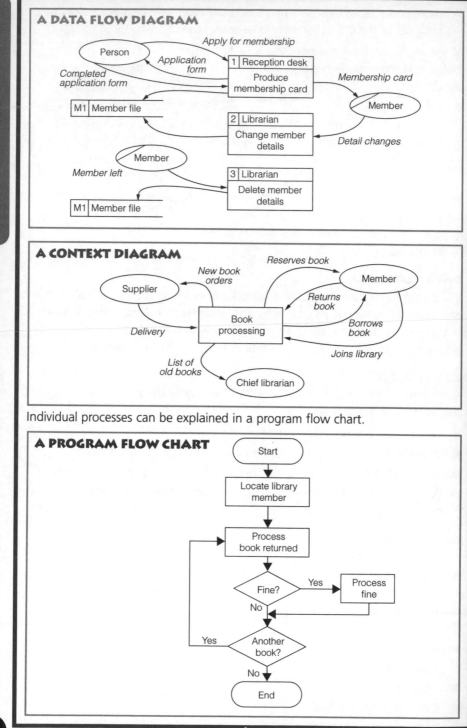

A DATA FLOW DIAGRAM

Apply for membership

Person

Application form

1 | Reception desk
Produce membership card

Completed application form

Membership card

Member

M1 | Member file

2 | Librarian
Change member details

Detail changes

Member

Member left

3 | Librarian
Delete member details

M1 | Member file

A CONTEXT DIAGRAM

Reserves book

New book orders

Supplier

Member

Returns book

Book processing

Borrows book

Delivery

Joins library

List of old books

Chief librarian

Individual processes can be explained in a program flow chart.

A PROGRAM FLOW CHART

Start

Locate library member

Process book returned

Fine? — Yes → Process fine

No

Another book? — Yes

No

End

INPUT

To get the output you need requires the right input. You should make and describe your plans about how the data is to be input. In most cases, this will mean some screen forms with spaces for data to be typed in. It might refer to particular regions on a spreadsheet. As with the output, you should make some decisions on what screens you need and make sketches of how they might look.

PROCESSING

Here, you need to explain what will be done to the data. This may include selection of material to go into a newsletter and laying it out with choices made about fonts and positions. In the case of spreadsheet projects, you will need to mention the calculations and other manipulation that will be needed. Database solutions will require some mention of updates and queries.

MENUS

Some projects will be based on a menu system. If this is so, you should make a diagram to show how each menu option leads to the next. This process may be suitable to show the routes through a website.

PROTOTYPES

One very useful process that happens in real-life situations is that the developer makes some prototypes of the proposed system in order to show the client. These are non-functional screens that give the client an idea about how it will look. This provides an opportunity for feedback. You could make some simple screens, either with the software of your choice or by sketching them by hand or with word-processing software. Include feedback from your client.

BACKUP STRATEGIES

All computer systems should have a backup strategy in case the data is lost or gets corrupted. Often, this need be no more than a statement that all files will be burned onto a CD every day. It may be more sophisticated such as an incremental backup, where only updated or new files are backed up. Don't forget to include a strategy for the storage of backup and how files might be restored if necessary.

Design

The easy way to understand what design is all about is to think of it as a **detailed** set of plans that could be handed to **someone else** who could then set up your system. Many projects have poor designs that can be spotted simply because they fail the 'can someone else read this and do it?' test.

What has to be designed?

You must design everything that you are going to produce.

In the analysis stage, you should have identified the outputs, inputs and processing required. You therefore have to create a design for:

- each of the outputs
- each of the inputs
- each of the processes.

SUB TASKS

It is important all the way through your projects, just as it is in real-life projects, to break the job down into sub tasks. This makes what seems to be a big job into small pieces that are manageable and not nearly so scary.

RETROSPECTIVE DESIGNS

Many students make their systems and then **retrospectively** produce designs. It is especially tempting to do this with database projects because each part of the system can be viewed in design mode as it is being produced.

Tip The best projects look as if they were **first** planned and **then** implemented.

THE CLIENT

It is best if the client is involved in the design process.

Some awarding bodies insist on this if a candidate is to score top marks.

The idea is that as the parts of the system are designed, the client is invited to comment on the designs to see if they meet with approval.

This means that you should include a range of designs for some of the parts, followed by decisions and changes made as a result of the client's comments.

Your work should include some **rejected** designs.

TEST PLANS

All projects have a section on testing.

It is helpful if at the design stage you appreciate what testing is for. It is not just to 'make sure that it works'. Testing is a deliberate attempt to show errors.

The tests need to be planned, i.e. designed, so that all aspects of the solution are put through the testing process. You need to plan tests that can generate definite, provable results. If your project does not seem to fit in with a test plan of this sort, you should think again about your choice of project.

TEST DATA

You should decide in your design section what data you will use for test purposes.

Remember that it should test all aspects of your system and should cope with any error that the user might make.

You should include:

- **normal data** – the system should accept data of the type that is expected
- **boundary data** – make sure that the highest and lowest acceptable values are accepted, but values beyond these are rejected
- **erroneous data** – data that is of the wrong type should be rejected.

VALIDATION

Most computer systems benefit from validation routines.

Validation routines are checks that the system makes on any data **as it is being input**, to make sure that it is **reasonable.**

Validation does not prevent users from making mistakes, but it can reduce these errors.

There are many ways to provide validation. Examples are:

- setting a data field to be a particular data type so that numbers, for example, cannot be entered
- choosing data from a list or combo box so that only an acceptable set of choices is available
- setting up check boxes to make choices
- setting up templates so that only certain layouts are possible.

Validation not only reduces avoidable errors, it gets you marks as well.

Moderators are always on the lookout for plenty of validation.

A sub-heading 'Validation' makes sure that it gets noticed.

weather : Table

Field Name	Data Type	
Date	Date/Time	
Wind Speed (kph)	Number	
Wind Direction	Text	
Precipitation	Number	
Pressure	Number	
Relative Humidity	Number	
▶ Temperature	Number	▼

Microsoft Access ☒

⚠ Temperature outside range

[OK]   Help

weather

▶ Date	1/01/2000
Wind Speed (kph)	12
Wind Direction	SW ▼
	SW
Precipitation	S
	N
Pressure	NW
Relative Humidity	NNW
	NE
Temperature	NNE
	W

General	Lookup	
Field Size	Long Integer
Format	
Decimal Places	Auto
Input Mask	
Caption	
Default Value	0
Validation Rule	>-30 And <50
Validation Text	Temperature outside range
Required	No
Indexed	No

Implementation

This is your 'product'. Implementation is where you put the system together.

You do this according to all the plans that you set out during the design stage. The moderator won't see your implementation, so this section is more particularly about **proving** that you have done it and proving that it all works.

With some awarding bodies, the implementation section also includes testing. In this book, we shall treat testing separately.

In real life, the word 'implementation' can mean two quite different things. It can mean:

- the programming of a computer solution, or generating one by using one of the many **application generators**
- the **roll out** of the system, where it is delivered to the customer, installed and set to work.

GCSE projects are mostly about the first meaning. However, it can be a good idea at least to show some awareness of the second meaning.

How clever is your project?

We have seen that moderators need to work fast in order to get their work done in time. One judgement that they have to make straight away is whether your project is 'substantial'. This judgement is made mostly by looking at the implementation, because the implementation is the 'product' that you have made.

In the implementation section, it needs to be very clear that you have used a range of techniques. Don't just go for the usual ones. Use techniques either from within one software package, or from a range of several types of software.

It might help to think about the software you use from two different perspectives, the user view and the developer view.

THE USER VIEW

Most people who work with computers use standard software in their work at least some of the time. That normally means Microsoft Office. They write documents, make newsletters, set up simple spreadsheets or may even put together a flat file database. They are simply using a tool from a toolbox.

A flat file database has only one table.

THE DEVELOPER VIEW

A software developer will produce a new application for others to use. Better projects take the developer approach.

Be discriminating

It is important that you show off clearly what the product can do without distracting the reader with too much, and maybe irrelevant, material.

Everything you put in must have a purpose. Also, everything in it must have comments or a heading so that the reader is left in no doubt about what it is.

Important **Tip**
– every printout, screenshot, file dump and other output should have some form of comment or heading explaining what it is.

So, what actually goes into this section?

This depends upon the nature of the project, but some of the following should be there.

- Demonstrations of some of the printouts that the system can produce. Don't forget – these must be annotated so that it is clear what they are.
- Screenshots of output screens such as enquiry results
- Demonstrations of input – screenshots showing data-input screens that are empty and some with data entered
- Screenshots of menus
- Screenshots of warning messages when validation rules have been broken
- Screenshots of components, as in databases, in design view
- Program code with full comments. This may be full listings if you have done a programming project or it may be short routines that the application generator has produced for you. If this is the case, still comment on it
- HTML coding with comments

- Printouts of spreadsheet formulae
- Mail merge templates and a **sample** of merged letter or other document
- Graphs
- Empty templates
- Templates with text or graphics in place
- Preliminary attempts to produce a screen form or document
- Final improved versions of forms or documents.

Here are some rules about implementation

Bad implementation	Good implementation
No screenshots or printouts	Proof that every part of the system works
Lots and lots of printouts with no particular purpose	Carefully selected printouts that are chosen to illustrate a particular aspect of the system
Large file dumps (the entire contents of a database)	Selected output to show a particular feature of the system
Automatic dumps of default values in a database	Selected information about values that you have changed for a reason
No annotation	Clear annotation that is 'to the point'
No resemblance to the design	Product has clearly been developed from the design
No evidence of development	Some record of error correction

Testing

If you take care of the testing section, you will put yourself ahead of the rest!

Some of the best students often neglect to test their work properly. Maybe this is because it can often be boring going through all the bits that you have already done and know that they work.

Real-life testing

It may help – as usual – to think about how IT projects work in real life. Remember that many IT projects are big, complicated and expensive. You should also realise that many real-life IT projects go wrong. When they go wrong, it can cost literally millions to put things right. Many IT projects have been abandoned after wasting huge amounts on them.

Projects go wrong because:

- there was insufficient understanding about what they had to do
- they were insufficiently tested.

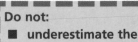

Do not:
- **underestimate the importance of testing.**

What is testing?

We have already seen that testing is not just some vague idea of 'seeing if it works'.

Testing is a deliberate attempt to 'break' the software or other solution. It is **supposed to** find faults. If a test finds a fault, then it is a good test.

In real life, the testing is usually done by people who are not the original programmers or developers. The people who made the system have probably become a bit too close to the work and may not want to see it fail.

You might even want to get someone else to have a go at finding errors. Even if you don't fix all the errors, a good testing section will show some up.

Lots of projects list many tests with a remark by each one such as 'it worked' or just a tick. This is hard to believe! Did this project get to this stage without any faults at all? You should report the failures – this is what testing is all about.

What should be tested?

Some things can be tested and some cannot.

For example, you can test the following:

- If you have made a spreadsheet solution to a problem, you can work out what the results should be if you enter a particular figure. You can go through all the stages with a calculator and check that you have got the formulae right and the right answer comes out.
- In a database project, you can check that adding a new record results in the new data appearing in a query.
- In a website, you can test the links.

But, it's not always so straightforward. What if you have made a newsletter for your project? How do you test that? The answer is – you can't if it is just a one-off. Some students try to 'test' documents and other one-off products like posters and logos by asking people's opinions of them. They sometimes get them to fill in questionnaires, asking such things as 'is it colourful?' This is not testing – this is evaluation.

Testing is objective. In other words, if two people carried out exactly the same test on your software, they would get exactly the same result.

If your project leads to a testing section that seems to be completely subjective – just a matter of opinion – then you have not chosen a project that will lead to the higher marks.

It is possible to make a solution testable if there is some active data processing going on. For example, in the case of the newsletter, a project could centre on making a template that can be used again and again in order to produce other newsletters that conform to the same format. You can then test this to see if, when the template is used on another newsletter, the sections of the letter are all laid out according to the desired style.

How much testing?

Ideally, you should test every action that your solution can carry out. In reality, though, you may have a solution that has just too many aspects to it. If this is the case, then you can test representative parts of it to demonstrate to the moderator that you know how to test. For example, if you have a website with lots of links, there is no need to demonstrate that every single one of them works. You just need to convince the moderator that you know how to do tests like this.

Types of test

NAVIGATION

Many projects have forms that lead to other forms, or menu items that lead to actions taking place. Website projects have hyperlinks that lead to other places. Database projects have buttons that lead to the next record. A sample of whether these work should be included in the tests – for example, you could include a table and image like the following.

Test no.	Part of the system to be tested	Test action	Expected result
30	'What's New' text leads to 'What's New' page	Click 'What's New'	'What's New' page opens in browser

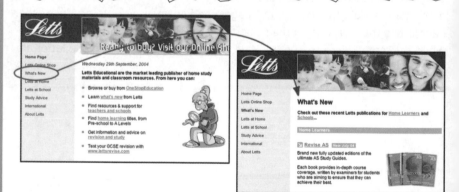

DATA AMENDMENTS

All database projects and many others such as spreadsheet solutions need to be tested to uncover errors in data processing. At the very least, there ought to be tests to ensure that data can be added, deleted or amended within a database.

This will normally be shown by presenting output before and after a change has been made.

CALCULATIONS

Any aspect of your project that has calculations should be tested against known results produced by hand or by calculator. As usual, the report can simply include a sample of these.

FUNCTIONALITY

If your solution is supposed to produce some effect, such as operate a motor, a sample of these should be included. You can include photographs in your evidence if necessary.

Reporting your tests

In the design section, you will probably have planned a series of tests to check each aspect of your work. You can re-use the grid that you made there with extra columns and when completed, put that in your report.

Test no.	Part of the system to be tested	Test data	Expected result	Actual result	Page ref (evidence)
1	Customer name input	J8nes	reject	message 'letters only' displayed	31
2	Customer name input	Jones	accept	data accepted and added to the customer table	31

The pages where the evidence is displayed should show the results very clearly. You can do this most easily by numbering the tests and also numbering the outputs.

Action as a result of testing

We have seen that tests show errors and you should not be shy about reporting these. If you have made amendments as a result of picking up errors, you should include some comments about this. Very few students do, so put some in and make sure that you bring it to the moderator's attention with a bold heading.

User guide

> Not all specifications require you to produce a user guide so you may be able to leave out this section.

If you have already seen some professional user guides this section will be easier. Make sure that you have looked at a variety of manuals and installation instructions. If you haven't got any of your own, ask your teacher to show you some that come with the software belonging to your school.

Activity
Another way to find user guides is to look at the websites of software manufacturers. For example, details about Microsoft Word can be found at: http://office.microsoft.com/en-gb/FX010857991033.aspx

■ User guides are very varied. They range from a very brief set of instructions on how to get up and running, to detailed coverage of every aspect of a system.

■ User guides also come in all sorts of different forms. There are still paper manuals, but increasingly, instructions are provided on CD, as 'help files' within the application or on the Web. For the purposes of GCSE, you will need to produce a paper one so that the moderator can read it easily.

■ User guides are also designed for different users.

1 Mass-produced software – A mass-produced product like Windows normally comes with brief instructions even though it is probably the most complicated software in the world. This is because most Windows users don't want to know much about it – they just need it to be there doing what it has to do. Those who need to know more will buy books on the subject and subscribe to information sources such as the Microsoft knowledge base.

2 Specialised software – This will normally have more detailed instructions as these will be part of the deal when the software was ordered. There will not be lots of books about a piece of software or a computer solution that is only in use in one organisation.

Tip
You need to think about who is going to read the user guide.

Know your audience

Tip

Your user guide is about **your** solution to a problem, not about the software you used to produce it.

- You can assume that your reader is reasonably bright and already has some computer knowledge. This is important because you must not waste time describing how to use a well-known software product like Access. Your user guide is about using **your** product, not someone else's product such as Microsoft's.

> If you have produced something as a one-off such as a single newsletter (not a good idea!), you will already have seen that you can't test it. Similarly, you can't have a user guide for it either! So, make sure that your solution is aimed at someone else to use – that way you can have a user guide!

- It is helpful if you at least think of your user guide as a stand-alone document, even though you will probably present it with the rest of your documentation. Think of it in sections and it might even help if you make a brief contents page for it.

What goes into the user guide?

This varies according to the project, but some sections will be common to most projects.

SYSTEM REQUIREMENTS

Outline the specification of the computer equipment needed to run your solution. This should include both hardware and software. The hardware should be fairly well specified and might say something like:

- processor 2.5 GHz or better
- 256 Mb RAM
- at least 80 Gb hard disk
- CDRW drive
- 14" monitor
- laser printer

The software might be

- Windows XP Professional
- Access 2000 or later

INSTALLATION

The user should be told how to put the solution onto his or her own computer. This will probably mean explaining how to copy the files and to what directory.

HOW TO USE

This is the most obvious section. Whatever functions are provided they should all be explained one by one, possibly with examples and screenshots to demonstrate them.

ERROR MESSAGES

If you have incorporated any of these (you may have put them into data-field validation processes) you should list them and explain what to do about them.

TROUBLESHOOTING

You may be able to anticipate some mistakes that people might make and put in some quick fixes.

FAQs

You can anticipate some questions that users might have and put in the answers in an easy to use question and answer format.

BACKING UP

Most systems need some form of backing up routine. You can make suggestions about how to do this – possibly by using Windows Explorer and comment on how often and to what media.

Evaluation

All projects have to be evaluated. This means assessing how well the product does what it originally set out to do.

This is not the same as testing. Testing involves checking that the parts work. Testing is repeatable. Evaluation is more a human reaction or an overview – a measure of satisfaction with the product.

Evaluation ought to be done mostly, but not entirely, from the client's point of view. After all, what matters in the end is whether the client is satisfied with the product and is likely to come back for repeat business.

Tip

The best evaluations will contain feedback from the client or the users.

Evaluate against the specifications

Back at the beginning of the project, you set out a requirements specification. This is a detailed description of what the client wanted. Ideally, it should have been a bullet point list. There may well have been more general objectives such as 'to improve the security of the data'.

Each one of the objectives and the specifications should be looked at in the evaluation. For every single one, you should make some sort of comment. The comment can be in general terms if it is simply a matter of expressing a degree of satisfaction.

An example of the sort of comment to make could be:

'The software should allow customer details to be looked up by customer number or by name.
It is possible to look up the customer by number or name and it is also possible to browse through the customer records in order to find a particular customer. A search screen is provided where various search criteria can be entered.'

Feedback from the client/user

Any comments from those who actually use the product are valuable. These can take various forms.

LETTERS

If you can get a genuine letter from your client that comments honestly on the system, this is one of the best ways to evaluate the system. You can then go on to make comments on the client's reactions and perhaps how you could improve the system in the future.

Your report should contain remarks such as:

> *'Data entry was easy and the software has already reduced the number of errors by 50% compared with our old system. However, some of our users found it difficult to find their way around the menu system and needed quite a lot of training before they could handle it confidently.'*

If you do include letters, make sure they are *specific* and *relevant*. Do **not**, as some students do, include pointless remarks such as: 'This was the most wonderful thing that has ever happened to our business. Thank you so much for transforming our lives.' This will not gain you marks.

QUESTIONNAIRES

These can be valuable. They can be set up to cover the important aspects of the system that you, the developer, want to know about. They are particularly useful when:

Tip If you do use questionnaires, only include a few just to show how they work and possibly to summarise the overall findings.

■ you have a number of users whose opinions you want

■ you are assessing something intangible such as the user-friendliness of a product

■ you want to get some opinions about particular alterations you have in mind for future products.

Do not:

■ **include dozens of filled-in questionnaires as it just looks like a desperate attempt to make a lot out of not very much information.**

Further extensions

Hotel Booking System

User evaluation

1. How often do you use the system?

Every day ☐   Once a week ☐   Less than ☐
                                         once a week

2. Rate its ease of use on a scale of 1 – 10 (1 very difficult, 10 very easy)

☐

3. On a scale of 1 – 10 (1 poor, 10 excellent) rate the following features of the software:

Interface ☐

Speed ☐

> No software product remains static.

Developers are always improving them by making them easier to use, adding extra functionality or improving their performance. You should think ahead and include ideas for future extensions that might be included in version 1.1.

It's worth trying hard with this. Spend some time thinking of some useful and realistic extensions, rather than simply saying things such as 'I would add more pages to the website'.

Good ideas for extensions could be:

■ the user interface can be made more friendly by responding to feedback from the users

■ an extra module can be added to produce the staff wage slips

■ a data export feature could be added to the spreadsheet to update the company report automatically.

Word processing and DTP projects

The next part of this book will look at how to get the best results from different types of project and help you make decisions where you have the choice.

Word processing and DTP projects are treated together, because they are both concerned with document processing.

If you are doing a small project such as one in the Edexcel collection, then making one of them document processing makes sense. However, if you are doing just one major project, it may not be a good idea to focus on this area. It can be difficult to bring in enough techniques to make it substantial. Also, most people can handle software like word processors quite easily and there are only limited possibilities for customising the software effectively to make what is a new product. Remember, in some specifications you will have to produce a user guide.

You will have to think hard if you want to produce a substantial major project with document processing. Because documents are static things, it is too easy to do a project that doesn't do very much. You therefore need to put in lots of clever features that actually do things to help users.

NEWSLETTERS AND SIMILAR IDEAS

A basic idea that can form the start of a document-based project is a newsletter. The comments about this apply equally to any other document that you might choose to produce. Similar examples can be advertising brochures, catalogues and children's story books.

We have already looked at how it is not a good idea to produce a 'one-off' in a GCSE project. So, avoid *just* making a newsletter. A newsletter will work as a project if you add extra functionality or other parts to it.

Tip

Don't make the documents too big. Once you have shown that you can make a well-constructed document, there is no point in doing it again and again and by adding more pages. You want lots of features, not lots of similar pages.

The best way to make a project out of a document such as a newsletter is to:

- work on making a template so that lots of similar newsletters can be produced in some consistent house style
- produce a **range** of documents including the newsletter so that you have some data-processing functionality. This could mean customising the newsletter for different readers by using mail-merge techniques or by sending out letters with the newsletter that are themselves customised.

Techniques to look at

GCSE ICT projects are about making systems for people to use. They should make life easier for someone or improve the quality of some document.

Most users of word processors are only ever aware of about 20% of the software's capability. To make a good document-processing project, you need to look into some of the remaining 80%. There are some obvious areas to explore.

Tip

It can be a good idea if your starting point for a document-based project is not so much 'what it will be about' but 'what techniques will go into it'.

MACROS

Macros really help to:

- reduce work
- ensure consistency.

For example, if a secretary needs to enter a standard phrase in a standard font throughout a document, a macro is the answer. If you look at some Windows documentation, you will see expressions such as *Microsoft Windows* ™ in many places. If you had to type this many times it would be a great nuisance to have to use italic, type in the whole product name and add the trademark sign in superscript. A macro can deal with that in one key press. You can probably think of lots of short cuts like that.

TEMPLATES

A template can be a real time-saver. If you produce some of these so that a number of documents have a similar 'look and feel', that can be useful 'added value' to a word-processor package.

Templates in DTP can include standard layouts using predetermined frames, fonts, colours, borders and a host of other design features.

MAIL MERGE

This is the obvious addition to any word-processed or DTP project. It is possible to use this with either type of software and this opens up a lot of possibilities for customising a solution for a client. Don't forget that mail merge is not just about producing personalised letters. It can be used to make any standard document with variable parts such as labels for anything, school reports and invoices.

EMBEDDED AND LINKED OBJECTS

A document such as a company report may need to include a graph. If this graph is linked rather than embedded, the document can be reproduced whenever the underlying data is changed and that way the graph will be updated.

Spreadsheet projects

Spreadsheets are mostly used for manipulating data (although they can be useful for storing static data, too), so they present many opportunities for producing solutions to problems. Even so, quite a lot of students do not exploit them enough to qualify for higher marks.

Choose something flexible that can have new data entered in it and produce new results.

> **You should avoid doing a spreadsheet project that consists only of lists of data with some simple calculations. Shopping lists are no good – even if they are big shopping lists with lots of expensive items!**

Models

- Models are mathematical relationships that attempt to represent real life.
- Spreadsheets are ideal ways to make models on a computer.
- There are unlimited ways to use these, ranging from costing up an event such as a wedding to modelling the economy of a country in order to decide on tax levels.

What if?

You should be very familiar with the use of spreadsheets to test hypotheses and work out what will happen if something is changed. You can set up a set of relationships – as complex as you like – that let you answer questions such as:

- What if I increase the prices of all my products by 10%? Will this generate enough profit to cover my expenses?
- What if I leave my lights on when I go out? How much will this increase my electricity bill?
- What if I get rid of the car and go everywhere by public transport? Will I save money and if so, how much?
- What if the supermarket opens one more checkout to reduce queues? Will it be fully occupied and pay for itself?

Tracking data

Anything that produces a set of figures over a period of time can be good material for a spreadsheet project. Good examples are:

- the performance of shares in someone's portfolio
- weather data
- population figures for humans or another species
- data from data logging experiments.

The nice thing about ideas like this is that the figures can be linked in real time to a graph for easy and instant understanding.

> Real-time operation is where the output from a system occurs immediately after the relevant input.

Booking systems

You can set up a spreadsheet so that the cells are narrowed to make small boxes. These can be used to represent seats in a theatre that change colour (use conditional formatting) when the data is changed. The sheet can be set to count the booked seats and work out income if required.

Techniques

As with document projects, you should carefully consider a range of techniques over and above the obvious in order to make the project ambitious enough.

MULTIPLE PAGES

A new spreadsheet file starts with three pages (worksheets) by default. Many people never get beyond using just one page. It is as easy to reference data on a different sheet as it is on one sheet, so making use of multiple pages can help organise your project better. You can have sales data on one sheet with a price lookup table on another one.

FORMULAE

Nearly every spreadsheet project will make use of formulae. Make them easier to work with by naming cells instead of always referring to them by their coordinates.

FUNCTIONS

Everybody knows about SUM and AVERAGE to make calculations easier to set up. Don't forget that there are many functions in any spreadsheet software.

Take a look at them some time to see if you can use some less obvious ones.

MACROS

Macros are a rich source of potential for a spreadsheet project. Think of any repetitive action such as formatting a sheet in a particular way or plotting the same graph again and again, and you have an opportunity to build in a macro to help the user. If you assign the macro to a keyboard shortcut or a menu button, it makes the spreadsheet even easier to use.

CONTROLS

You can put all sorts of controls on sheets to make them easier to use. Obvious ones are combo boxes that get their data from some part of the work book or command buttons to activate a macro. You can see what is available by selecting View-toolbars-control toolbox.

FORMS

You can create forms, just as you can in database applications and make things easier for the user.

SPREADSHEETS AS DATABASES

The row and column layout lends itself to making simple databases. You can set up part of a sheet to store data this way, and then set up a data form to make it easy for your users to enter and search for data.

GRAPHS

Graphs are so easy to do with spreadsheets, you will often find a way to make good use of them. Consider pasting them into a word-processed document and linking them to the spreadsheet so that the graphs are always updated.

Presentation

Bear in mind that it is easy to use cell formats, colours, alignment and many other features to make your spreadsheet easy to read.

Make sure that in your implementation, you include (annotated) shots of your spreadsheet to show it in display formula mode so that the moderator can see how you set it up.

Database projects

Databases are by far the most popular projects. If you are doing a set of small projects, you will have to do one. If you are doing one major project, you will be well advised to do one.

Databases make a good safe choice for project work because:

- they are crucially important in the 'real world'
- they offer a wide variety of techniques to make your project ambitious
- they more or less force you to include all the things that you ought to include anyway
- it is usually fairly clear when you have done enough.

Don't allow the dangers in database projects to put you off, but do think about them.

- You can be over ambitious and take too long.
- You can waste a lot of time entering lots of data, although you don't need to. Only enter enough data to demonstrate the capabilities of the system.
- Some things that you will probably want to do require a lot of experience.
- Be prepared to keep your timing under control. You may have to allow some time for learning a new piece of software.

> Database projects mean Microsoft Access for most candidates.

This allows you to do a substantial and realistic project with plenty of scope for a good analysis and design.

Database projects are nearly all 'relational databases'. In the real world, these predominate, but they are not the only model.

> Relational databases are made up from more than one data table.

Real-life relational databases may be made from dozens or hundreds of tables.

At this level, you ought to be looking at between three and five.

One table is not enough. Three is ideal – it allows you to work with relationships without getting bogged down with too many entities.

Choice of subject

You should be led by the complexity required for a good grade. If you work with three tables and do a good job, you can easily get top marks. If you are more ambitious than that, you could get in a mess with timings and still not get a higher mark.

VIDEO RENTAL SHOP

Three tables means three entities. So, the old favourite – a video rental shop – is absolutely ideal. You can substitute other lending or hiring activities if you want.

The three entities are
- the videos
- the customers
- the loans.

Tip

This scenario works very well for a database project, but you may not wish to use it. You may want to assert your individuality by working on a scenario that you are particularly interested in.

With this, you get the chance to do a useful link between the video_id in the video table and the video_id in the loans table. You do the same to link the customer_id to the loans table. (Maybe at this stage rewrite in normal English instead of field names and use the video reference number in the video table and the loans table. You do the same to link the customer reference number in the customer and loans tables.)

STOCK CONTROL PROJECT

Another scenario that is just right is a stock-control project. You can then have a stock table, a supplier table and, if you want to be more ambitious, you can add a transaction table. This could be split even further if you wanted lots of items on one transaction or bill, but you are getting into A/AS level territory then.

What goes into a database project

One of the attractions of doing a database project is that there is not much argument about what has to go in. This saves you having to agonise too much! Microsoft Access makes it easy for you – it provides a number of objects to manipulate a database and you should make use of at least four of them.

TABLES

Without tables, you have no database. We have seen that you should try and create a situation that needs about three of them. Tables are handy for another reason. You really ought to include plenty of validation in a database project.

You can set up validation rules and restrictions on data entry when you set up your tables. It is easy and definitely notches your project into a higher level.

FORMS

These make the user interface for your project. The user doesn't want to see the actual tables. Forms let you make things friendly by putting buttons and other controls for navigation and other action purposes.

QUERIES

These let you select data in any way you want. That's what databases are for – no one ever wants to see the entire contents of a database, just like no one wants to read all the names and numbers in the phone book! All relational database projects need queries. Don't forget that there are different types of queries. Some can do calculations and summaries, others let you add data to a table.

REPORTS

These are the printed output. They can be lists, grouped in any way you want or any other useful output such as invoices or school reports. They can be based on any number of tables or queries, so the possibilities are endless.

Other useful things

MACROS

Macros in Access are a bit different from macros in spreadsheets and word processors. You can't record them. But, they are very simple and are useful if you want a very straightforward set of things to happen as the result of (usually) clicking a button.

EVENT PROCEDURES

These are chunks of program code that are run as the result of an event, such as – guess what – clicking a button, or pressing Enter. Many simple ones can be generated automatically and if you want to tinker with them to make them do more exactly what you want, this is not difficult.

EXPRESSIONS

These are ways to make your database even more flexible. You can use expressions – on queries, for example – to capture data from another location and then use it. You can make a query get its condition from a field on a form so that it behaves differently under different circumstances. Expressions can do calculations so that, for example, a form can display someone's age by looking at date of birth data in a table.

Website projects

Website projects can be very ambitious and impressive. They can also be very trivial. Make sure that yours is a substantial one!

There are some fairly well-known 'extras' that you need to consider to earn your website an A*–C grade.

> **Do not:**
> - **just do a simple website with pages that are all much the same and just a few links between them. This is not ambitious enough, even if there are lots of pages. As always, we need some clever stuff and added functionality.**

Audience

You have to have a very clear idea right from the beginning about who your site is aimed at and what you want to achieve with it. This might be new customers whom you want to contact you in order to expand the business.

Too many websites are **just there** because their authors thought that they needed to be there, but they don't have a clear purpose.

Organisation

A good website consists of:

- web pages
- resources.

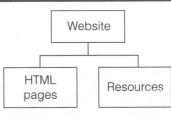

> The web pages are the HTML files.

You will create these using an HTML editor or maybe – if you are ambitious – an ordinary text editor like Notepad.

> The resources are going to be files that your web pages need.

These will usually be image files or they could be script file or style sheets.

The layout should be documented in your design section.

> **It is important to organise these items properly. You will need a folder to hold the website and at least two subfolders to hold the pages and the resources. If this is not organised right from the start, you will find that the site does not work if you upload it or transfer it to another location.**

LINKS

All websites contain links – either with the site or to other sites.

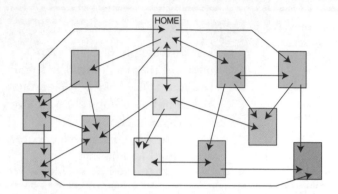

Decide what links you need right from the start.

MAPS

You need a site map in your design.

This shows how all the links will fit together. You would be surprised how many students do not do this.

BUTTONS

Buttons are a main feature of websites.

It is easier to make buttons with web authoring packages. Try out a variety of types.

GRAPHICS

These should be saved as JPEG or GIF files in your images/resources folder.

Do not try to paste images in.

TABLES

These are absolutely vital to website projects.

You cannot drag and drop items anywhere on an HTML page. If you divide your page up into table cells you can drop your text blocks and your images exactly where you want them.

STYLES AND THEMES

It is really easy to make a plain website look good by introducing a theme. Web-authoring software such as Front Page can make this very easy.

FORMS

Use forms to get feedback from the user. You may need to have access to the web server to make them work.

VALIDATION

Try to validate at least some of the input to a form.

At least two computers have to be in communication to make a website useful. The web server holds the pages and supplies them to the user, who is working on a client computer. Any processing done by the server is called server-side processing and any that is done by the user's machine is called client-side processing. Most GCSE website projects tend not to include much server-side processing because of the need to have access to the web-server computer.

Other projects

You probably have freedom to make projects from other software resources apart from the ones already looked at. Edexcel specifies a spreadsheet and a database project, but the others can be free choice.

Presentations

Presentations are an easy way to make a multimedia project.

Remember that multimedia means including at least three of:

- text
- graphics
- sound
- moving pictures.

These are always popular, partly because they make it easy to make a product that looks good. But, because they are easy, there is the danger that they will be trivial as well. As usual, to make a project worth a high grade, you need to put in a good range of techniques. Presentation software is not as 'feature rich' as other applications, so there is not so much to think about.

Tip

Don't forget – you can save a presentation as an HTML file – it might be a good starting point for a website project.

Many presentation projects tend to be trivial and do not score the highest marks. A set of slides with a few bullet points and pictures that simply move from one to the next is not showing enough skill for a good grade at GCSE.

Think about using some of these:

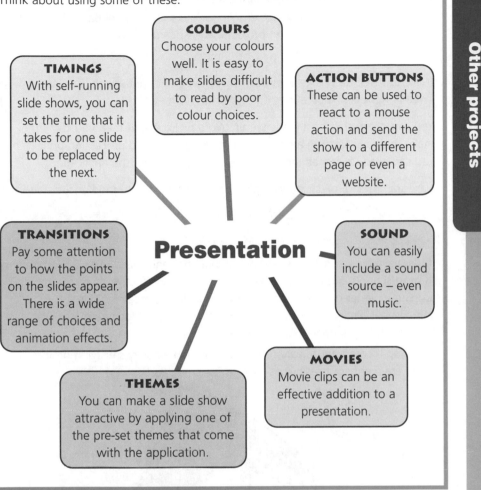

COLOURS
Choose your colours well. It is easy to make slides difficult to read by poor colour choices.

TIMINGS
With self-running slide shows, you can set the time that it takes for one slide to be replaced by the next.

ACTION BUTTONS
These can be used to react to a mouse action and send the show to a different page or even a website.

Presentation

TRANSITIONS
Pay some attention to how the points on the slides appear. There is a wide range of choices and animation effects.

SOUND
You can easily include a sound source – even music.

THEMES
You can make a slide show attractive by applying one of the pre-set themes that come with the application.

MOVIES
Movie clips can be an effective addition to a presentation.

Programming

It is a shame that so few projects are based on programming. It is not difficult to learn how to program and it is also a lot of fun.

With a programming project, you can show off a wide range of techniques and put your project well ahead of the rest.

It can often be easier to write good, complete documentation with a programming project because the stages in the specification work very well with program development.

PROGRAMMING LANGUAGES

The easy way to write software for Windows is to use Visual Basic. This opens up a huge range of interesting project ideas, such as making:

- a calculator
- a quiz or game
- teaching aids.

Microsoft Office has its own built-in version of Visual Basic. It is called VBA – Visual Basic for Applications.

You can get at this most easily within Word or Excel and then you can either make the programming a part of a spreadsheet or word-processing project, or you can produce something more or less separate from the applications.

Programming projects provide perfect scope for writing good analysis and design sections.

CONTROL AND DATA LOGGING

If you have access to the necessary equipment – and this should be no problem in most schools and colleges, you can make a very effective project from logging weather or science data and possibly later processing it in a spreadsheet. Projects of this type are relatively easy to document as well, because the component parts are clear.

Fixing up a computer to various devices can make a very satisfying project. There are plenty of possibilities such as:

- buggies and robots
- lifts
- level crossings
- car parks.

A great advantage of projects like these is that so few students do them. It is another way to make your project a bit special.

Dave's DVDs

We are going to look at some parts of a database project. A real project would take up more space than there is room for in this book so only extracts are shown here. The business is called Dave's DVDs. It is an easy-to-follow problem that covers a lot of techniques and is just the kind of thing you need to do to get a good grade.

A rental or lending system like this is an extremely common scenario for database projects. It has a minimum of three data tables and makes use of most of the other features available in a relational database manager such as Access. You should come up with your own ideas and use this example as a guide to the sort of things that need to go in.

Vary things by choosing different scenarios and making your project carry out some different actions. Remember, in order to get the best grades, you need to produce clear and thorough documentation. The project needs to be reasonably ambitious, but it does not have to be spectacularly clever!

Dave's DVDs: Identification of the problem

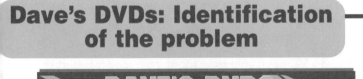

It really helps to decide on a name and location plus a bit of history.

Dave's DVDs is a DVD rental shop in Neasden. It was started as Neasden Video Hire by Dave Smart in 1995 when Dave realised that there was a gap in the market in this area. Originally, Dave rented out video films and computer games but as the popularity of DVDs increased rapidly in recent years, Dave has found that there is more profit to be made with them and he has changed the name of his business to reflect this.

At the moment, Dave works in the shop himself and also employs four assistants so that the shop can be open from 9am until 10pm every day.

We now set the scene for some of the data fields to be used later.

He does not have a computer system at the moment and relies on a paper-based filing system that has to keep records of the DVDs he has in stock and the members who have rented them out. He has to be careful that the DVDs are rented out in good condition so that when they are returned, he can see if the member has scratched them or damaged them at all.

Dave and his assistants are often asked if they have a particular film in stock. Sometimes, members don't know what film they want to watch and they might ask for a general type such as a recently made action thriller.

Many members get annoyed with all the bad language that there is in modern films and they ask if there are any films that don't have that.

All the members have to fill in a membership form when they first start using the service and Dave needs to know basic details such as their names, addresses and phone numbers as well as their date of birth, as some DVDs are age-restricted. Dave then issues the member with a membership card and asks the member to choose a PIN for security purposes. Obviously, this PIN is not written on the card, but Dave keeps a record of it.

Dave now has about 500 members on his books and he has over 10,000 DVDs for hire, with about 200 being out on hire at any given time.

The business is doing well and more members are joining every day. A new business park is due to open shortly and Dave expects lots of the people who work there will want to hire DVDs during their lunch breaks to take home with them in the evenings.

The current paper-based filing system is just not working effectively any more and Dave knows that a computer-based system is needed to help him expand the business efficiently.

This is setting the scene for calculating storage space later.

PROBLEMS TO BE SOLVED

1   Dave finds it hard to keep track of all the stock that he has. Sometimes, this has resulted in theft and non-return of items on hire.

2   When a new DVD is received from the supplier, someone has to fill in a record card with the details of the DVD. This is taking far too long and diverts staff from serving the customers.

3   When a new customer registers as a member, it takes a long time to fill in a record card for the customer.

4   When a member changes personal details, the record cards have to be altered and some of these are getting very messy.

These problems must be solvable by computer and be specific so that you know when you have solved them.

5   It takes ages to find out if a particular DVD is on loan as all the record cards have to be looked through.

6   Members sometimes lose their membership cards and new ones have to be written out.

Dave is also worried that if a disaster happened, such as a fire or burglary, he could lose not just his stock, but all the valuable data about his members.

OBJECTIVES

Dave has been interviewed and after much discussion, it has been decided that he needs a system that will, at the very least, have the following capabilities:

1   Allow quick recording of the details of new DVDs. A new DVD should take no longer than two minutes to enter into the system.

2   Keep track of where each DVD is at any given time.

3   Allow quick booking out and return of DVDs. This should take no longer than one minute.

4   Allow quick registration of new customers and the amending of their details.

5   Print membership cards.

6   Allow a quick search of members' details.

This is close to a requirements specification and will form the basis for everything you do, right up to the final evaluation. Notice that some of the objectives are **quantitative** – success in these can be measured.

7   Hold the necessary details for 50,000 DVDs and 2,000 members, to allow for expansion of the business.

8   Make it easy to back up the data.

ALTERNATIVE SOLUTIONS

There is more than one way to approach Dave's problem.

1 STAY WITH THE PAPER-BASED SOLUTION

Advantages

- There will be no need to invest in computer hardware and software.
- There will be no need for any extra expensive training.
- The system exists already so there will be no 'down time' during changeover.

Disadvantages

- As the business grows, the problems of data access will grow.
- Mistakes will continue to be made, damaging the effectiveness of the business.
- Not future proof.

2 STORE MEMBER AND DVD DETAILS IN A SPREADSHEET FILE

Advantages

- This requires very little effort to set up.
- Details can be backed up, answering one of Dave's concerns.
- It is easy to re-order data and make chart summaries if required.

Disadvantages

- It is not possible to connect the data about DVDs, members and loans in a meaningful way.
- Some data will be stored in more than one place, such as the details of DVDs in stock and on loan. This will lead to mistakes and inconsistencies.
- Future expansion will not be easy with such a basic system.

3 SET UP A RELATIONAL DATABASE

Advantages

- The data about DVDs, members and loans can be held just once, in separate tables.
- The tables can be linked so that data can be displayed as required.
- Queries can be used to extract whatever details are needed.
- Reports are available for any printed output.
- It is much easier to expand the database in the future, because the existing tables do not necessarily have to be redesigned.
- There are lots of tools available for producing an easy-to-use interface.

Disadvantages

- The solution will take longer to put together.
- Considerable work will have to be done to set up the database objects.

CONCLUSIONS

In order to give Dave the best possible product that will serve all his needs effectively now and into the foreseeable future, a relational database will be produced. Microsoft Access provides all the tools needed to make this.

Most of the staff are familiar with Windows-based solutions and there are plenty of cheap training courses for those who need extra help.

> You need to give a reasoned account of possible alternatives. The rejected alternatives must be fairly reasonable ones.

Analysis

OUTPUTS REQUIRED

> You should make preliminary drawings of proposed screens and indicate that you have shown them to the client for comments.

SCREEN

Member details, individual and lists

Search for DVD results (answering enquiries about DVDs)

Display overdue DVDs

PAPER

Report of all overdue DVDs

Overdue DVDs

Date due	DVD ref	DVD Title	Member ref	Surname	Forename	Title	Telephone
09/06/2004	6	Terminator 2	5	Brown	Harriet	Miss	0234333
15/06/2004	1	Sleepless in Seattle	1	Smith	Fred	Mr	01234567
16/06/2004	3	Funny things	4	Kennedy	Karl	Dr	078787878

Report of DVD loans

Membership card

Dave's DVDs Membership Card

Member ref	5
Forename	Harriet
Surname	Brown
Age category	Adult

> It is often easiest to start with the outputs because this is, after all, what the client wants the system for. Once these have been decided on, the inputs and processes required are often more or less decided for you.

INPUTS REQUIRED

The following input actions will be required.

You will probably think of rather more inputs and outputs than are given here.

You can make the basic ideas up on a computer, but there is no doubt that many moderators do prefer a hand-drawn version.

ENTER NEW MEMBER

This process will be carried out when a new member registers. The member will give the details directly to the assistant who will type them into the database.

Fields needed: member number, name, title, address, telephone number, PIN and date of birth for each member.

ENTER NEW DVD

This process will occur when a new delivery of DVDs is received. The details will be entered into the database as the DVDs are unpacked.

Fields needed: DVD number, title, genre, age certification, language content.

EDIT MEMBER

This process will occur whenever a member's details change, notably in case of change of address.

LOANS DETAILS

These details will be entered when a DVD is rented. The details will be edited when the DVD is returned.

Fields required: DVD number, member number, date issued, date due back, date returned.

SEARCH DVD

There will be a screen that allows a search to be made by title, number or genre.

The inputs will all be done by entering the details at the keyboard. Later developments will enable loans and returns to be done by bar code scanner.

VERIFICATION AND VALIDATION

The member details entered into the system will be printed out to give to the members to verify that the details are correct.

The DVD information will have validation on certain fields where there is a simple choice to be made such as the category of DVD.

USER INTERFACE

The user will see a main menu screen when the software starts up. This contains buttons that lead to the screens where details will be entered and results displayed.

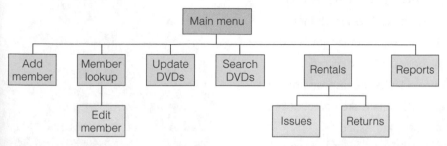

DATA FLOWS

ISSUING A DVD

When a member is borrowing a DVD, the details of the member and the DVD required are looked up in the relevant tables of the database. If there is no record of the member, a new record is set up.

The details of the loan are recorded in the loans table. The following Data Flow diagram shows the loan process.

This is one of several places where including the correct type of flow charts is beneficial. It clearly shows how the parts of the system work together. You should make plenty of flow charts to show the most important activities. They not only communicate your ideas to the reader, they help you to organise your ideas better.

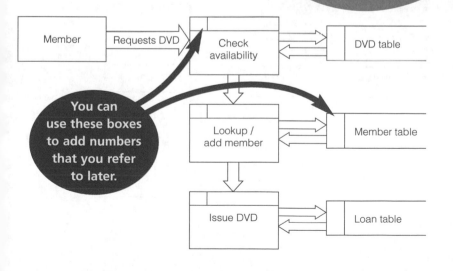

You can use these boxes to add numbers that you refer to later.

PROCESSING

System flow charts are often a good way to illustrate processes.

During the operation of the DVD system, data is processed when:

- new members are registered
- members' details change
- members' details are being looked up
- new DVDs are recorded
- old DVDs are disposed of
- DVD details are being looked up
- loans are issued
- loans are returned
- reports are produced.

There is lots of processing to cover in this project. It includes updating records in all the tables, searching for individual members and DVDs and the production of reports. You would normally draw diagrams to illustrate a wide range of these, but there is only space here for some examples.

You should use the proper symbols for all flow charts and keep the labels in them to a minimum. See figure below of the proper symbols.

COMMON SYSTEM FLOW CHART SYMBOLS

Keyboard input

Disk storage

Data storage

A process

Paper output

DATA-FLOW DIAGRAM SYMBOLS

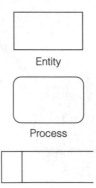

Entity

Process

Data store

SYSTEM FLOW CHART FOR REGISTERING A NEW MEMBER

When a new member is being registered, the system will be able to check some of the details to avoid data entry errors. The basic process is shown in this diagram.

SYSTEM FLOW CHART FOR DVD ENQUIRIES

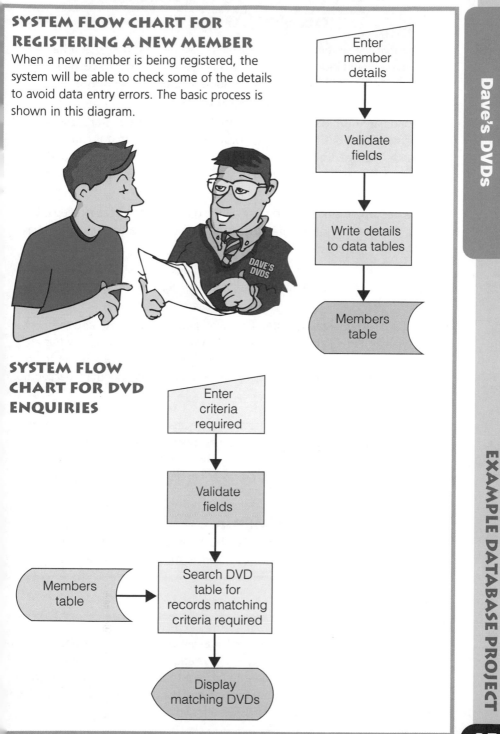

Enter member details

Validate fields

Write details to data tables

Members table

Enter criteria required

Validate fields

Members table → Search DVD table for records matching criteria required

Display matching DVDs

Backup and security

The data that the system is storing is vital to Dave and his business. If he were to lose it, he would lose contact with his members and it would cost a lot to start again. To avoid this, there must be some sensible backup processes organised. There are a variety of strategies you can use.

- Second hard disk: Have a second hard disk that mirrors all transactions. The advantage of this is that there is always a second copy that is completely up to date. The disadvantage of this is the extra expense of the drive and that if data were damaged by a virus or some operator error, the mistake will be duplicated to both copies.

- Tape backup: It is possible to store all the data on a small tape called a DAT tape. This holds a lot of data but it is a slow process to backup a large hard disk and to restore data from a tape.

- CD: A CD writer is a quick way to make a back up of all the data from this system. If a rewriteable disk is used, it will be possible to do very quick backups.

- Total and incremental backups: A total backup of all the data and the software in the database would not take very long while Dave only has a small number of members. As the business grows, it might be better to do an incremental backup, where only the files that are changed are backed up.

HOW OFTEN?

Ideally, backups should be instant so that there are always at least two copies of the important data. This would be too time-consuming for the assistants, so it is recommended that the business data is backed up to CD every evening after the close of business. That way, if a disaster happened, only one day's trading details would be lost.

STORAGE OF BACKUP MEDIA

It is recommended that the backup CD should be taken off the business premises so that in case of fire or theft, there is still a copy in safe keeping.

Software

The software to produce a solution for Dave will be a relational database manager created with Microsoft Access. Its relational database capabilities will allow the amount of redundant data to be kept to a minimum. This will reduce the likelihood of any of Dave's staff making mistakes. All data items will be held once only, except in the case of fields used for links.

Hardware

To start with, the system will be implemented on a stand-alone computer. It will be a desktop computer with:

- 1 GHz processor
- 128 Mb RAM
- 20 Gb hard disk
- 100 mbps network card
- internal CD-ROM
- CD writer
- colour ink jet printer

This set up is sufficient to run Windows XP as well as Access and provides enough storage space for all the files that will be required.

The network card may as well be purchased with the computer as it is probable that the system will expand to occupy a small network if the business succeeds as hoped for.

The CD writer will be used for making regular backups.

Design

The system for dealing with Dave's DVDs is a relational database and the software necessary to process it. It will be made from:

tables – to store the data

forms – to make a user interface

queries – to find data and link the tables

reports – to produce printed output such as membership cards.

In addition, the forms will have buttons on them to help the user perform the necessary functions. There will be a small amount of program code behind these buttons to make them do what is necessary.

> The thing to keep in mind throughout the design section is that there should be enough detail for someone else to be able to produce the solution.

Tables

There are three entities to this system – the members, the DVDs and the loans. The relationships are one to many – each member can have many loans and each DVD can be rented out many times.

> In any database project, the design section has to include the table structure. It is surprising how many projects leave this out.

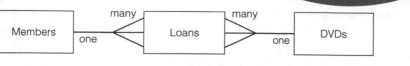

Members —— one —< many Loans many >— one —— DVDs

A separate table will be created for each of these entities – the members, the DVDs and the loans.

The size of each field is recorded so that the disk space needed can be calculated.

Each number field will normally, by default, take 2 bytes and text fields will be as many bytes as there are letters.

MEMBER TABLE

Field name	Data type	Size (bytes)	Comment	Validation
Member_ref	Number	2	Primary key	Setting this as primary key automatically prevents duplicates.
Surname	Text	20		Automatic length check
Forename	Text	20		Automatic length check
Title	Text	4		Choose from list box
Age_category	Text	5		Choose from list box
Telephone	Text	14		Length check
PIN	Text	4		Numbers only
Total record size		**69 bytes**		

DVD TABLE

Field name	Data type	Size (bytes)	Comment	Validation
DVD_ref	Number	2	Primary key	No duplicates
Title	Text	30		Automatic length check
Genre	Text	15		Choose from list box
Bad_language	Yes/No	1		Check box
Age_category	Text	4		Choose from list box
Damage	Text	20		
Date_acquired	Date/Time	8		Must not be in the future
Total record size		**80 bytes**		

LOAN TABLE

Field name	Data type	Size (bytes)	Comment	Validation
Loan_ref	Number	2	Primary key	No duplicates
DVD_ref	Number	2	Foreign key	
Member_ref	Number	2	Foreign key	
Date_rented	Date/Time	8		Entered by system – today's date
Date_due	Date/Time	8		Must be in the future
Date_returned	Date/Time	8		
Total record size		**30 bytes**		

Forms

THE MAIN MENU FORM

One form is set up to act as a main menu or 'switchboard'. It will contain buttons that lead to all the other main functions and one to quit the application. The basic layout will be as in this plan.

Each button will be attached to an event procedure that opens the relevant form.

The layout of each form should be presented here, either as a hand-drawn plan or you can use graphics software to produce a plan. You should not give screen dumps of forms that you have already created. This is supposed to be a **plan**.

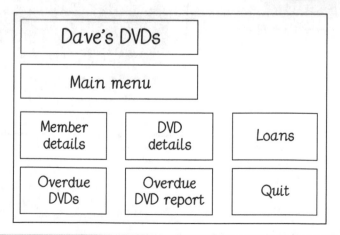

Dave's DVDs

Main menu

| Member details | DVD details | Loans |
| Overdue DVDs | Overdue DVD report | Quit |

FORM FOR EDITING DVD DETAILS

Most of the fields will be entered into text boxes. These are bound to the relevant fields in the data tables. The age category and genre fields will be selected from list boxes.

A command button activates an event procedure to take the user back to the main menu. The name of the button is cmdMainMenu.

The name of the main menu form is MainMenu.

The event procedure is:

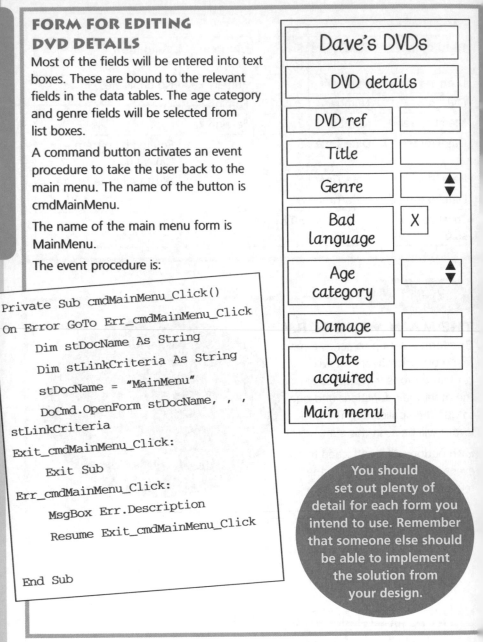

Dave's DVDs

DVD details

DVD ref

Title

Genre

Bad language   X

Age category

Damage

Date acquired

Main menu

```
Private Sub cmdMainMenu_Click()
On Error GoTo Err_cmdMainMenu_Click
    Dim stDocName As String
    Dim stLinkCriteria As String
    stDocName = "MainMenu"
    DoCmd.OpenForm stDocName, , '
stLinkCriteria
Exit_cmdMainMenu_Click:
    Exit Sub
Err_cmdMainMenu_Click:
    MsgBox Err.Description
    Resume Exit_cmdMainMenu_Click

End Sub
```

You should set out plenty of detail for each form you intend to use. Remember that someone else should be able to implement the solution from your design.

Queries

Queries will be used to find particular members or DVDs. A query will also be used to find any DVDs that are overdue and this can be used to print out a list of these DVDs together with the names and telephone numbers of the members who have them. This list can then be looked at so that the relevant members can be telephoned as a reminder.

OVERDUE DVD QUERY

This query will be based on all three tables. It will take the DVD name from the DVD table, the customer name and telephone number from the customer table and the loan details from the loan table.

In order to find which DVDs are overdue, the criterion <now() is put into the QBE (query by example) box under the date_due field. This will show all the details needed for contacting the member for all rentals where the return date is 'less than', i.e. earlier than today.

QUERY FOR PRINTING MEMBERSHIP CARDS

Sometimes it is necessary to print a new membership card. A query is set up to find a particular member. This is based on the member table and includes the following fields:

Member_Ref

Forename

Surname

Age_category

Dave's DVDs Membership Card

Member ref	5
Forename	Harriet
Surname	Brown
Age category	Adult

In the criteria field, the expression

`=forms!member!member_ref`

is entered. This way, when a particular person's record is selected, clicking a button to print a new membership card can activate a report, which in turn activates this query. The query finds only the one record that matches the reference number currently being displayed.

Reports

Reports will be used to provide printed output. The main reports needed are:

1 A list of all overdue DVDs

2 Printed membership cards.

> You will probably want other reports. Usually it is best to base them on queries so that only certain records get included.

OVERDUE DVD

The layout of the overdue DVD report has been planned in the Analysis section but, in consultation with Dave, improvements have been made.

PRINT NEW MEMBERSHIP CARD

When a member's details are showing, a button lets the user print a membership card for that person. A report is set up to do this and it is based on the query that selects just that one member.

Test plan

When the database application has been completed, the following tests will be carried out.

Test no.	Part of the system to be tested	Test data or action	Expected result
1	Navigation from main menu to member form	Click	Member form opens
2	Add new member	Mr John Johnson, adult member, telephone number 0123426353525352	Telephone number will not be accepted – it is too long
3	Add new member	Mr John Johnson, adult member, telephone number 01234263535	Should be accepted
4	Print membership card	Choose member No. 5	Should print a new membership card for Harriet Brown only.

> These are just some examples. There should be plenty of tests planned, which must include some that involve selecting certain records and entering, changing and deleting data.

Implementation

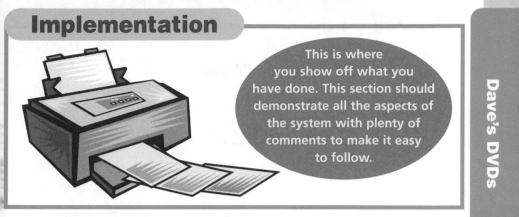

This is where you show off what you have done. This section should demonstrate all the aspects of the system with plenty of comments to make it easy to follow.

The data tables

Three data tables have been set up to contain the data about the DVDs, the members and the loans. The structure of the DVD table is shown here.

You can repeat this process with other tables, but do not waste space showing lots of data. If the tables are similar, a selection will be enough.

DVD : Table

Field Name	Data Type
DVD_ref	Number
Title	Text
Genre	Text
Bad_language	Yes/No
Age_category	Text
Damage	Text
Date_acquired	Date/Time

General | Lookup

Field Size	Long Integer
Format	
Decimal Places	Auto
Input Mask	
Caption	
Default Value	0
Validation Rule	
Validation Text	
Required	No
Indexed	Yes (No Duplicates)

The next screenshot shows the table with some data entered.

DVD : Table

DVD_ref	Title	Genre	Bad_language	Age_category	Damage	Date_acquired
1	Sleepless in Seattle	Romance	☐	12	None	10/10/2002
2	Nasty stuff in LA	Horror	☑	18	None	10/10/2003
3	Funny things	Comedy	☐	12	Slight scratch	12/12/2003
4	Pretty things	Comedy	☑	12	None	12/12/2003
5	Terminator	Action	☑	15	None	10/10/2002
6	Terminator 2	Action	☐	15	None	10/10/2002
7	Casablanca	Romance	☐	12	None	10/10/2002
0			☐			

Forms

THE MENU

When the system is started, the main menu appears.

The menu screen is made from a number of labels and command buttons.

Clicking on any of the buttons takes the user to the required screen. All other forms have buttons that lead back to the main menu.

The start up option was used to make sure that this form always appears when someone starts up the software.

FINDING MEMBER DETAILS

When the member details button is clicked, the members screen appears.

Each member's record can be looked at in turn by using the record selector at the bottom of the screen.

The member screen is composed of text boxes, labels and command buttons. One leads back to the main menu, the other is for printing a membership card.

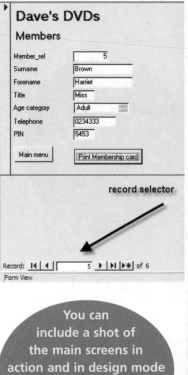

record selector

You can include a shot of the main screens in action and in design mode with a description of how they were constructed.

74

Queries

The structure of the query for finding all overdue DVDs is shown below. The criterion field under Date_due is set to <now(), which finds all DVDs that were due back before today.

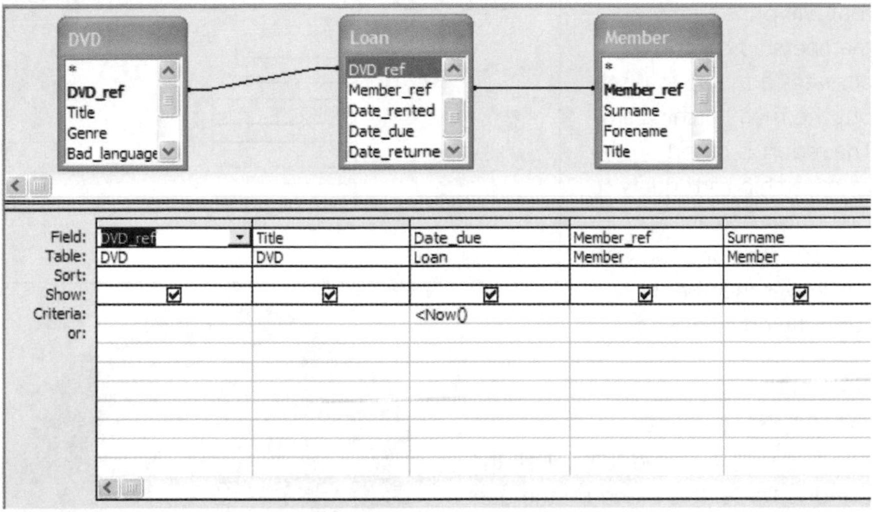

There is a query for selecting a member's record to print a membership card. Its structure is shown below. The query selects only one member record, the one that is currently showing in the members form. The criterion

```
[forms]![member]![member_ref]
```

looks at the collection of forms, then the form called member then the data in the field member_ref to find the member to look up.

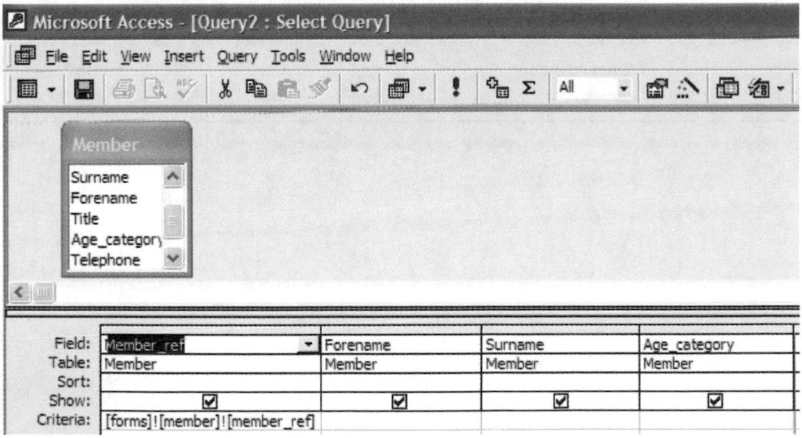

Reports

PRINTING A MEMBERSHIP CARD

There is a button on the members' details screen that will print a new membership card. This activates a report that sets out the membership card. The report is based on the membership card query so that only one card is printed – the one for whichever member is currently on display.

Dave's DVDs Membership Card

Member ref	5
Forename	Harriet
Surname	Brown
Age category	Adult

PRINTING A LIST OF OVERDUE DVDS

Another report is used to print all the overdue DVDs. It is based on the query that selected them.

Make sure that all the capabilities of your solution are documented, illustrated and explained. You do not need to do a lot of writing, but enough to make everything obvious.

Overdue DVDs

Date due	DVD ref	DVD Title	Member ref	Surname	Forename	Title	Telephone
09/06/2004	6	Terminator 2	5	Brown	Harriet	Miss	0234333
15/06/2004	1	Sleepless in Seattle	1	Smith	Fred	Mr	01234567
16/06/2004	3	Funny things	4	Kennedy	Karl	Dr	078787878

Testing

This is a separate section in some specifications. In others it may be part of the implementation. Most of the testing can be presented as a table, with page references to where the evidence may be found. If you have already presented screenshots in your implementation, you can refer back to them.

Test no.	Part of the system to be tested	Test data or action	Expected result	Actual result	Page no. of evidence
1	Navigation from main menu to member form	Click	Member form opens	member form opens	xx
2	Add new member	Mr John Johnson, adult member, telephone number 01234 26353525352	Telephone number will not be accepted – it is too long	Telephone number not accepted	xx
3	Add new member	Mr John Johnson, adult member, telephone number 01234 263535	Should be accepted	Accepted	xx
4	Print membership card	Choose member No. 5	Should print a new membership card for Harriet Brown only.	Printed the correct membership card	xx

There should be a wide range of tests.

It is good if you can include some tests that did not work out. You can then report how you made corrections and fixed the problem.

Evaluation

The rental system for Dave's DVDs performs all the tasks originally planned for it.

1 Allow quick recording of the details of new DVDs. A new DVD should take no longer than two minutes to enter into the system.

This is now possible, once the users have got used to the system.

2 Keep track of where each DVD is at any given time.

By looking at the loans table, it is easy to perform a search on any video to see if it is out or has been returned.

3 Allow quick booking out and return of DVDs. This should take no longer than one minute.

This is now possible. Previously, this took at least three minutes

4 Allow quick registration of new customers and the amending of their details.

The members screen allows member details to be amended and added very quickly.

5 Print membership cards.

Any member can have a new card printed in a few seconds by clicking the button on the members screen.

6 Allow a quick search of members' details.

This can be done quickly by using the search facility, but it would be better if member names and numbers were presented in drop-down boxes so that they could be searched for very quickly by either field.

Future enhancements

If Dave gets on well with this system, it would be a good idea if the searching process were made easier with drop-down boxes for both DVDs and members.

It would be a good idea too, if a report could be produced showing which DVDs were the most, and the least, popular over the last year, so that decisions could be made about future purchases.

SYSTEM REQUIREMENTS

You need a computer system with at least the following specifications:

1 GHz processor   128 Mb RAM   20 Gb Hard disk

FOR BACKUP
CD writer

FOR HARD COPY
Colour Ink Jet printer

SOFTWARE
Microsoft Access 2000 or later

> You may or may not have to include one of these. It depends on the specification. It is a good idea if you try to approach this as an entirely separate section, as if you were making a separate booklet.

INSTALLATION

1   Create a directory in a convenient location and name it DVD.

2   Insert the distribution CD.

3   Copy the file DVD.mdb from the CD to the directory.

All the necessary parts of the database will now be installed.

STARTING UP

You can either use Windows Explorer to find the DVD file and double click on it, or you can drag the file to the desktop. You will then have a short cut to the software.

The main menu screen will appear.

ADDING NEW MEMBERS

From the main menu screen, click the Member details button. This will bring up the member screen, which will be showing the first record.

At the bottom of the screen is the record selector.

Click on the Add new record button.

You will then get a blank record where the new member's details can be entered.

Member

Dave's DVDs

Members

Member_ref	1
Surname	Smith
Forename	Fred
Title	Mr
Age category	Adult
Telephone	01234567
PIN	0989

Main menu   Print Membership

Add new record

Record: 1 of 6

A list box lets you choose what category of membership is correct for the new member.

If you need to print a membership card at this point, you click on the button to do so.

Dave's DVDs Membership Card

Member ref | 8
Forename | Sarah
Surname | Harvey
Age category | Adult

Dave's DVDs

Members

Member_ref | 8
Surname | Harvey
Forename | Sarah
Title | Miss
Age category | Adult
Telephone | 0998899889
PIN | 1898

Main menu | Print Membership card

Record: 7 of 7

Click the main menu button to return to the menu screen.

MAKING A BOOKING

From the main menu, click the loans button. The loans screen will appear.

Loan | 1
DVD ref | 1
Member ref | 1
Date rented | 10/06/2004
Date due | 15/06/2004
Date returned |

Main Menu

You can describe all the other processes that will need to be carried out, with plenty of labelled screenshots. You should also include how to book DVDs back in when they are returned, a troubleshooting guide, how to do backups and a glossary.

Click the new record button on the record selector. You can then enter the details of the DVD, the member and the relevant dates. If there are any more bookings to be made, you can click the new record button again.